CALMS

A Guide to Soothing Your Baby

D1531422

Debby Takikawa, DC
Carrie Contey, PhD

Foreword by Phyllis Klaus, MFT, LCSW

The information in this book is not intended as a substitute for medical advice. If your baby is crying or distressed and you feel there could be a medical problem, please consult your physician immediately. The C A L M S method of communication is not intended to take the place of medical care, but it does continue to be useful to you and your baby during illness. It is a good way to reassure and to keep contact with your baby if he or she needs to go through medical procedures or endure the discomfort of being ill.

 Hana Peace Works
P.O. Box 681
Los Olivos, CA 93441

www.calmsguidetosoothe.com

ISBN: 978-0-9768735-2-5

Distributed by Hana Peace Works
805-688-9877

Printed in Singapore
Cover and Book Design by Croff Creative
Cover photograph by Fran Collin
Photographs are copyrighted and may not be reproduced without written permission from the photographer.

10 9 8 7 6 5 4 3 2 1

Dear Ryan & Ariella:
Hope this little
book will help you
to see your baby
and yourself in
a different light.
You are both learning
together on this new
chapter of your lives.
Love,
Mum/Jean

CALMS

A Guide to Soothing Your Baby

We dedicate this book to our families

and the real-life experiences of

relationships we've shared together.

Contents

Foreword

It is a pleasure to write the foreword for this special book. It is simple but profound, small but filled with important information. In C A L M S, Carrie Contey and Debby Takikawa help parents understand the needs, moods, changes, and rhythms of their infants. Parents learn how to help their baby move from being distressed to a calmer state.

There is wisdom in recognizing your own feelings when entering your child's world. Babies' responses are like a barometer to their parents' or caretakers' emotions. New research has shown that during the whole first year of life there are transfers in emotions and physiological reactions from the right brain of the mother to the right brain of the baby.

All emotional responses have value. All become available from the early development of the limbic system in the womb. Emotions are protective. When an infant is upset, it means that something doesn't feel right at a basic level of survival. Infants cannot put an intellectual meaning to their emotions; they can only feel them throughout their bodies. When overly upset their heart rate goes up, stress hormones increase, and their little systems struggle to handle what may appear to them to be danger.

Unlike us, an infant's system is more fragile. It is immature and doesn't re-regulate quickly. If a baby is stressed too long, he or she may look quiet, but in reality could be having a micro-depression. The immune system can be lowered, and other reactions, such as tummy aches, can occur. It is truly important to recognize "messages" from your baby when he or she is upset. These messages are not verbal nor understood intellectually by the baby; they are felt experiences. The baby needs your help to return to a more stable state. This book provides an easy-to-follow method to do this.

Contey and Takikawa, both knowledgeable caregivers, teach parents how to respond sensitively to their infants, by first being aware of their own feelings, and then by using simple ways to reduce stress, even under trying conditions. The authors show how to acknowledge the baby's experience through gentle mirroring and a variety of other useful methods that will help the baby return to a calmer state.

These thoughtful, helpful methods—checking in with one's self and taking a moment to settle, listening to what the baby is communicating, reflecting back what you are perceiving, then offering comfort—are the basis of good communication. When practiced, they allow parents to work together in mind, body, and emotion to validate a sense of self in the baby. This type of care creates deep and lasting bonds between parents and their children.

Phyllis Klaus, MFT, LCSW

Your Amazing Newborn

Bonding:
Building the Foundations of Secure Attachment and Independence

The Doula Book:
How a Trained Labor Companion Can Help You Have a Shorter, Easier, and Healthier Birth

Introduction

66 Around the time of birth, for a few precious moments, we are sometimes able to tap into something so ancient, primal and wise, that we are able to transcend our limited view of what's possible.

—Noah Wyle
Narration, *What Babies Want*, the movie

Welcome and congratulations on the arrival of your new baby. We are honored to share this book with you and hope it will provide guidance and inspiration during this tender time of life and beyond.

It is an exciting time to be a new parent. We know more about babies and development than ever before. In fact, there is a revolution taking place in the way we think about and care for babies. At the core of this transformation is the understanding that your baby is a person who arrived from the womb with likes and dislikes, feelings and opinions, and an incredible ability to understand and communicate with you. Pause for just a moment and think about the fact that your baby is a whole person. When you keep this in mind, it changes how you are with your baby.

This book is for parents as well as anyone who will be interacting with your baby. It is intended to be an accessible, concrete guide to understanding how to be with your baby in ways that support both of you as you create a deep and loving relationship right from the start.

C A L M S is a simple five step approach to support parents and caregivers to calming and communicating with their babies. The five steps of C A L M S are:

Check in with yourself.

Allow a breath.

Listen to your baby.

Make contact and mirror feelings.

Soothe your baby.

We have divided this book into three parts. In Part I, we will guide you through the C A L M S steps and provide the hows and whys of the method. We will also introduce you to Anna, Mike, and their baby Joshua to illustrate how C A L M S can be applied in real life. Part II will offer basic information about human development. And finally, in Part III, we offer the answers to some common questions about the C A L M S method. Please note that we have alternated the use of "he" and "she" in each section so that it feels personal to all readers.

We have had a wonderful time putting our hearts and heads together to create this book, which honors your baby and your entire family. We respectfully present these ideas to you and hope that our words will be helpful as you find your way into parenthood.

–Debby and Carrie

PART ONE

CALMS

Five Simple Steps to Harmony

> " Making the decision to have a child is momentous.
> It is to decide forever to have a heart go walking
> around outside your body.
>
> —Elizabeth Stone
> Author

Anna and Mike are the new parents of Joshua, who is now four weeks old. They had a long, hard labor and birth, but there were no serious complications; they came home from the hospital the next day. Joshua is an adorable newborn, with a little crest of black hair, pink cheeks, and sparkling eyes. From his first day at home, Joshua tended to be a bit sensitive about any changes in his routine, and would cry and struggle as he tried to go to sleep. He often woke up crying or fussy. In spite of this, he usually slept a lot and was able to soothe easily with breastfeeding, bouncing, and being carried in the sling. Although they were starting to feel the effects of sleep deprivation, Anna and Mike were having a wonderful time falling in love with this magnificent new baby. Life with Joshua suited them, and after two weeks of being home, Mike was sad about having to return to work.

Since Mike went back to work, Anna has been home alone with Joshua most days. At first, things went smoothly, but as the days go on, Anna has grown more tired and Joshua has grown fussier. The late afternoons have been particularly challenging for both of them. For several days now, Joshua has been crying for over an hour; none of Anna's soothing and calming techniques seem to be working. Trying to handle this alone has not been easy for Anna, and she is wondering if she is doing something wrong, maybe spoiling him with too much attention. She is beginning to lose her confidence as Joshua gets harder and harder to console.

Today is a particularly challenging day. She anxiously waits for Mike to come home. She wants him to realize that it isn't so easy to be home alone with the baby all day, and she needs relief from the afternoons of crying. Her shoulders are tight, her throat is constricted, and she is exhausted. This is not what she expected.

The minute Mike walks in the door, Anna greets him with, "Oh good. You're home. It's been a hard day, and I really need you to hold Joshua for a little while."

Mike's job is stressful, and he is tired when he gets home. He could use a few minutes to shift from work mode to baby-care mode, but he can tell Anna has been struggling for the last few days, and the stress is starting to get to him too. He feels pressured to dive right in. "Sure, honey, what happened, are you guys all right? How are things going?" He takes Joshua, lays him over his shoulder, and heads to the kitchen to get a drink of water. At this point everyone is feeling frazzled.

After several afternoons and evenings with a fussy baby, Anna and Mike are feeling overwhelmed. They are both beginning to wonder, are we doing something wrong? Is there something wrong with our baby? Why didn't anyone tell us it was going to be this challenging?

Whether your story is similar or quite different from Anna and Mike's, we want you to know that we understand what it is like to feel challenged by new parenthood. Most parents have times when they are unsure about what to do. Part of parenting is wondering what is right for your baby and what will help him grow up to be the best person he can be.

Your Parenting Journey

There are many parenting strategies to choose from, however no matter which one you pick, it is your relationship with your baby that matters most.

It is your relationship with your baby that matters most.

Her physical, mental, and emotional well-being are based on the way you connect and interact with her. Our current understanding of infant development very clearly indicates that healthy development depends on consistent, loving, respectful interaction. In writing this book, our intention is to provide you with the support and information you will need to begin connecting and communicating with your baby from birth. Although we are here to provide ideas about how to do that, as parents, you instinctively know your baby and what is right. Trust your feelings and follow your heart; listen to your inner voice. The quieter you get and the more you listen, the more you will know intuitively.

Shifting from Shushing to Listening

"Who is this baby, how can I be connected to this child, and how can I understand what he needs?" When you ask these questions you shift your awareness away from "What do I need to do to this baby to get him to be quiet and content?" toward "I'm in a state of learning about who this person is and what he needs in order to feel safe and secure." If you make the focus of your work as a parent to slow yourself down and tune in to your baby, you will discover that your baby is telling you what he needs.

The C A L M S protocol is designed to help you open up to trusting yourself and listening to your baby. Babies are much more sophisticated, sensitive, and communicative than we might think. Knowing how aware they are changes how we interact with them. This book is about how to make that change.

Safety First

Your baby's most basic drive is to survive, and her first need is to know that she is safe. When we think about how to take care of a crying baby, we often go through the checklist of feeding, diapering, and physical comfort. These are important considerations, but secondary to your baby's need for safety. That's why the first step to calming a baby is to let her know that all is well.

Your baby is tuning in to your feelings.

The catch to this is that although babies are more sensitive, communicative and aware than we have given them credit for, they are not operating out of intellect; therefore, this communication about safety must come in a form that your baby understands. Mere words will not convey this to her. Your little infant knows she is safe when she senses that you feel settled and calm.

Babies understand and actually mimic and internalize their parents' inner states by reading their subtle expressions and body language cues. Body language is a powerful means of communication and accurately conveys our inner feelings. If you are feeling stressed or unsettled, your baby is tuning into that. Because safety is the first need, nature has provided us with the survival mechanism of the ability to sense and react to how others are feeling. When you are calm and settled, your baby will know that she is safe, which will help her settle, too. This is why the first two steps of C A L M S are focused on you, not your baby. When you start to move toward balance, your baby feels you relax and she will begin to settle. This is the single most important thing you can do to begin the process of soothing your baby.

Acknowledging Your Baby

The next two steps create the kind of communication that affirms your baby's experience. Opening your heart, listening with all of your senses, tuning in to your instincts, and patiently hearing your baby's voice are all part of this process. Listening to your baby in this way acknowledges your baby and helps him to know that you care about what he is experiencing. Now that your baby knows that all is well and that you are willing to hear what he has to say, you will find that he is much more receptive to the fifth step, soothing. Soothing is the next level of need fulfillment, and includes food, comfort, rocking, play, and whatever else you have already discovered that he loves about life.

C

Step 1
Check in With Yourself

A

Step 2
Allow a Breath

L

Step 3
Listen to Your Baby

M

Step 4
Make Contact and Mirror Feelings

S

Step 5
Soothe Your Baby

Step 1

C A L M S

Check in With Yourself

When your baby is upset and you are not able to calm her, it can be quite stressful for everyone. Because a baby's cries are meant to evoke a response, it is normal to feel anxious and overwhelmed when you hear them. However, it can be much more difficult to calm your baby if you are not calm yourself. The first step is to check in with yourself, take a pause, and begin to identify your own feelings. Slowing your pace and accepting where you are right now is the key to being able to initiate change.

How to Check In

Checking in with yourself is the first step in the process of calming and connecting with your baby.

Ask some basic questions and be honest with yourself. Are you feeling:

Scared	Stuck	Distracted
Angry	Inadequate	Sad
Frustrated	Guilty	Stressed
Helpless	Hopeless	Irritable

If you are feeling any of these feelings, the next step is to pay attention to your body sensations. For example, if you are feeling sad, ask yourself, where do I feel sadness in my body? Your body carries information about your feelings that your mind does not normally recognize. Scan your body for tension and other sensations such as tightness, aching, heat, pain, tingling, prickling, or dullness. You might notice these feelings anywhere in your body, but the following areas are a good place to start: jaw, throat, shoulders, hands, stomach, pelvis, and heart/chest.

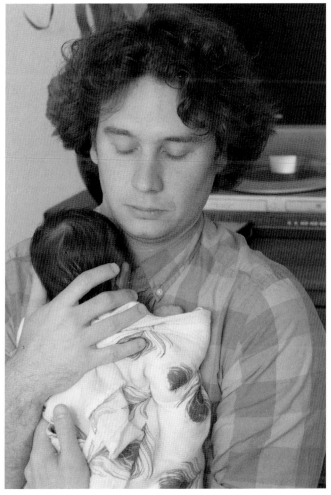

Just take it one step at a time.

Most parents experience tense feelings and un-comfortable sensations in these areas at some time or another. It's normal and natural to feel emotionally overwhelmed and physically uncomfortable when you are experiencing stress.

Acknowledging these feelings and finding the areas of tension are two ways to begin letting go of your stress. Just take it one step at a time.

Why Check In?

Your feelings form a bridge between you and your baby. Because your baby's cries can activate your own stress response, it is important to notice your stress and begin to understand it. Honestly acknowledging your feelings and sensations is a first step toward feel-ing calmer. Your baby will feel this shift because on an emotional level he is exquisitely tuned in to you. As you take this first step toward calming and settling yourself, your baby will notice the change and begin to settle with you. Taking this time allows you to establish mutual feelings of peace and love.

CALMS In Action

Checking In

When we left off with Anna, Mike, and Joshua, they were having a tough time. Sensing that they needed to do something to shift the mood, they start the CALMS steps. When Mike checks in with himself he realizes that he is exhausted, frustrated, and feeling ineffective. He notices his shoulders are hunched and his lower back is tight. He feels like he's lost his touch, and he wonders if Joshua only wants to be with Anna.

Meanwhile, Anna has started cooking dinner. As she checks in with herself, she realizes that the sound of Joshua's crying is evoking her feelings of anxiety. She's afraid to admit that she's worried that she's not a good mother, and wonders if she will be able to give Joshua what he needs. Her throat feels tight, her stomach is in knots, and she's on the verge of tears. Her inclination is to keep going and work on dinner but something inside of her says, "Just sit with the feelings for a minute."

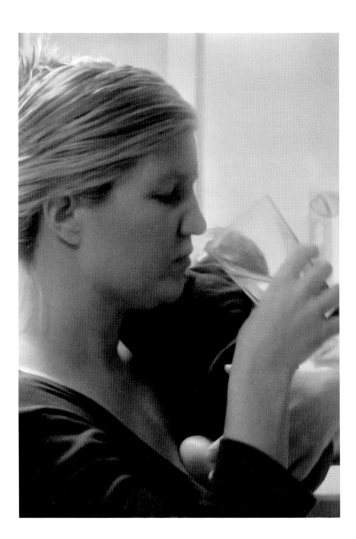

Step 2

C **A** L M S

Allow a Breath

Once you have checked in with yourself, take several deep breaths and allow things to simply be just as they are in this moment. Don't try to force a change. Trust that the change is coming. In the act of performing these simple steps, you are practicing "self-care" and intentionally calming yourself down. Slowing your body and mind and soothing yourself is a process. Different methods work for different people. We recommend trying some of the suggestions offered below and using what works for you.

How to Allow a Breath

You can allow yourself a breath with your eyes open or closed, sitting or standing, and just about anywhere:

- Deeply inhale for a four-count,
  and then exhale for as long as you can.

- Imagine that a sense of calm is entering
  and flowing through your body with
  each intake of breath.

- Do this three to five times,
  and repeat as needed.

Here are a few more ways you can practice self-care:

- Slowly drink a glass of water.

- Look out the window.

- Go outside for some air.

- Eat a healthy snack.

- Feel your feet on the floor.

- Tighten and relax your fists.

- Make eye contact with another adult.

- Get a hug or some physical contact from another adult.

- Call a supportive, empathetic friend or family member.

- Use positive self-talk: "I can do this." "My baby wants my help." "I am doing my best."

Sometimes getting to that calm place takes a few moments and many deep breaths. It may be necessary to turn your attention inward and away from your baby while you do these first two steps. As long as your baby is safe in your arms or on the bed, it is all right to take a few moments to care for yourself. This turning inward is an essential part of the process of calming your baby. She is feeling and reacting to your emotional states. When you feel tense, she feels anxious. When you feel settled, she feels safe. When you allow a breath and calm yourself down, she begins to breathe more easily as well. As she begins to settle, her body feels better, her stomach relaxes, and she receives better circulation for better digestion.

Focus on your heart.

Additional Exercises

Here are two more ways that you can practice slowing down and coming back to yourself:

- Focus on your heart and make space in your chest by inhaling again. Visualize the last time your baby was calm and asleep on your chest. Imagine the sensation of her warm little head on your chest and how good you felt, and take another deep breath.

- Imagine that your emotions and physical state are connected to an internal volume knob that you can slowly and gently turn down. When you are doing things to soothe your baby who seems to have a hard time settling, you can try turning down your "emotional volume."

Why Allow a Breath?

In the early stage of your baby's life, he is developing the ability to regulate his emotions. He is doing this in relationship with you. He is not equipped to settle alone. At this point, he needs and benefits from your help. Your baby is still forming and learning how to manage all of his emotional ups and downs. Because he is tuning in to you and your feelings, each time you go through an upsetting time with him, you have an opportunity to help your baby organize his emotions. When you stay connected with your little one and start to settle your own body, your baby will copy you. Taking a few moments for deep breathing and self-care during such times can be just what you both need to get back to a place of balance. When you are feeling balanced, you can be more effective in helping your baby settle, and feel safe and comfortable again.

CALMS In Action

Allowing a Breath

While holding Joshua in his arms, Mike allows a breath, and another, and another. He slips his shoes off and feels his feet on the floor. With each breath, his system settles just a bit. He also checks in with his body. He notices that his heart is racing and his shoulders are very tight. He specifically tries to focus his breathing into those areas. Mike reminds himself that right now he is feeling stressed and being with Joshua is a challenge. He also tells himself that he is a good dad and can take care of a crying baby. He continues breathing. This is not easy because Joshua is still crying, but he sticks with it.

Anna is appreciating herself for also taking a little pause and realizes that as she begins to breathe with her feelings, they dissipate. Her breathing deepens. She looks over to her husband and son and feels her deep love and appreciation for Mike and Joshua.

A

Step 3

C A **L** M S

Listen to Your Baby

Now that you have checked in with yourself and practiced a few moments of self-care, it's time to listen to your baby and to ask the question, "What are you trying to tell me, little one?" Your baby is a whole person with feelings and emotions; she is speaking a language that in some ways may be foreign to you. Her main way to communicate is through body language, facial expressions, sounds, and crying. You are learning her language, and although you may not immediately know what she is trying to say, it is very important to her that you are trying to understand what she is communicating. It might take some practice to feel proficient at deciphering her language, but trust that you will get there. You are one of the main people in her life, and she wants you to know what is happening and how she is feeling.

We know how challenging it can be to hear your baby crying and not understand what she needs, but by listening to your baby, you will be able to learn something about what she needs. This may be a new idea, a new way of thinking about parenting. It can be mystifying to communicate with this little person who does not speak your language. You are going to have to rely on your senses, observations, feelings, and intuitions.

Please note that the following listening and mirroring steps go hand-in-hand. You may find it useful to alternate back and forth between these two steps as the conversation develops between you and your baby.

L

By listening to your baby you will be able to learn what she needs.

The first step to listening is to become quiet inside.

How to Listen

Here are some simple tips for beginning the process of listening to your baby:

- Slow down.
- Become quiet inside.
- Use all of your senses to observe your baby.
- Pay attention to what your inner voice is telling you.
- Trust your instinct.

The first step to listening to your baby is to become quiet inside. Be patient, especially with yourself. Observe your baby's pacing, breathing, and body tension. Look at your baby and see the details of facial expression, body movement. Hear the sounds of the cry. Be willing to learn about your baby, and for the moment put aside the need to stop your baby's crying. Right now your job is to stay with yourself and to listen and watch your baby very carefully with an open mind. Give your baby time to express himself, and give yourself time to really take it all in.

Why Listen?

When you begin to understand what your baby is telling you, you can better meet her needs. Even if you don't understand her right away, your baby will be reassured to know that you are listening. When a small baby has genuinely responsive parents who see her as a person, it gives her a feeling of recognition and self-worth. The result is that she feels safe and loved.

New research has provided us with information about the complexities and awareness of babies, and how actively they are reaching out to connect with their parents. Even though they arrive in tiny, vulnerable bodies, we can interact with them. Although you and your baby are not speaking the same language, its true that your baby is trying to communicate her feelings and needs to you. She is intelligent and will try many ways to get you to understand her. The best you can give her is your respect and sincere effort to listen. As you sincerely listen and respond, you may find yourself in a new world of communication with your baby that can be quite remarkable and unexpectedly exciting.

CALMS In Action

Listening

As Mike's body starts to settle, and he turns his focus toward Joshua, he recognizes how vulnerable and frantic Joshua is feeling. Once he makes that shift from feeling inadequate into realizing that Joshua is having a tough time, he feels curious about what is happening for him.

"What's going on with you little man? How can I help you?" he says.

Joshua continues to cry but seems less frantic. Mike starts to realize that he is not causing Joshua's upset feelings, and this allows him to be more present. He thinks to himself, Wow, this little dude is really trying to tell me something.

Anna has started cooking dinner and realizes that Joshua's cry has taken on a different tone. He seems less upset. She can hear Mike talking to him and looks over to see what they're doing. Mike notices Anna and says, "Seems like he just wanted me to slow down and start listening."

L

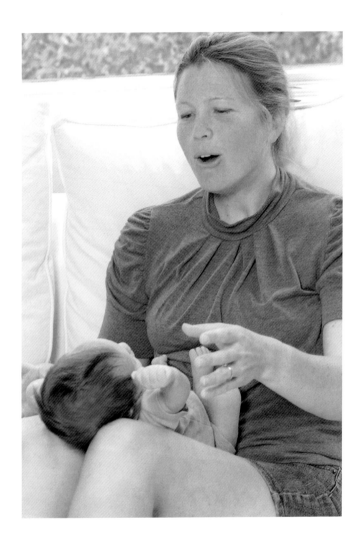

Step 4

C A L **M** S
Make Contact and Mirror Feelings

Now that you have reached this step, you are ready to interact with your baby in a way that you may never have considered doing before. Even though you have been talking to your baby, probably since before birth, now you are going to respond to your baby's cues. The previous step was to listen to your baby. Now you are going to take what you heard to heart and let your baby know not only that you have heard, but that what you have heard matters and is not trivial.

The variety of ideas presented here are only suggestions and possible scenarios. Listening and responding to your baby from your heart is what really works.

How to Make Contact and Mirror Feelings

Here are some simple ways to begin the process of making contact and mirroring what your baby is showing you:

- Think about what you hear, see, and feel as you observe and listen to your baby.

- Make comforting physical contact with your baby.

- Talk to your baby about what you think is going on.

- Leave your communication open-ended: "It seems like you feel . . ." or "It looks like . . ." or "I wonder if . . ."

Listening and responding from your heart is what really works.

- Keep the dialogue going by checking in again and noticing your baby's response to your words.

- Notice your own feelings and keep breathing.

- Continue cycling through the listening and mirroring steps for as long as it feels productive.

M

For example, you might notice that your baby is really scrunching up his face and holding his fists tight. You might say, "I see how scrunched up your face is and how tight you are holding your fists." When you have said that, it is useful to come back to the listening step. Your baby will respond to what you have just said. If you listen again, you will see what your baby does in response to being heard and reflected by you. It's a simple conversation, but it can lead to a lifetime of sharing! As you carry on this conversation with your baby, he will calm and settle, or if he has a complaint, he will be more able to maintain contact while he tells you about it. Most people know that you can talk to a baby, but what they don't realize is that the baby will answer.

Here are some examples of mirroring phrases that might be reflective. Keep in mind your baby will respond best when you reflect the movements you see and feelings you feel while listening to him. Your simple and genuine communication—the words you say and the way you say them, the expressions on your face and the way you move your body—conveys all of the information that your baby needs in order to understand your reflection:

"Oh, baby, you are having a tough time."

"I really hear you."

"Yes, baby, you are really upset.
   I see how upset you are."

"I see that your eyes are closed
   and your face is scrunched."

"I see how you are kicking your legs
   and moving your arms by your head."

"You seem really frustrated right now."

"That was a loud noise, and it startled you."

"I can see and hear that you are really crying."

"I see you looking at me."

"Wow, that's a big smile."

M

"Oh, looking away."

"That was a deep breath."

"Big stretch!"

You've been listening. You may not quite know what you are listening for or understand what your baby is saying; however, you don't need all the answers to begin to mirror your child's expression. Just a simple reflection of "Oh, I see your eyes are closed" might be enough to get the conversation going. The great thing about mirroring is that initially you don't have to know the meaning of the expression or movement. Just describe what you see. It's a tool for starting the conversation. You may not get all the information on the first try, but by getting even part of the message and mirroring it back, your baby will often have a distinct response of connection, excitement, or relief. As you let your baby know what you have seen and heard from him, keep on listening and watching for his response to what you are saying now.

Compassion builds communication.

The communication builds by going back and forth between listening and mirroring or responding.

Let your baby know you hear him and see how he is feeling. Be genuine and believe that your baby is trying to communicate. This step is about validating his experience and empathizing with him.

Although your baby might continue to cry as you are talking, you may notice that he is making more eye contact, or that the sound of the cry is changing.

Take time to find the connection.

Reflect this as well. In the case of eye contact, you might say in a pleasant but not overly playful voice, "Oh look, I see you looking at me," or "Hi there, little one," or "Thanks for looking at me." This kind of response keeps your baby in contact with you. Now that he knows you are watching him, he will try to give you more information.

Another thing that your baby might do is try to push away or hide his face. Respond to his body language. If you are trying to breast-feed and he is pushing away, you might tell him that even though you think he is hungry, you do not want to make him eat if he is not ready. Let him know that you are willing to wait, and that you have time to find out what he needs. Take your lead from his body language and the situation. As you practice doing this with your baby, you will be amazed to find out that you can carry on quite a complex conversation. Just keep on listening and reflecting back.

Why Make Contact and Mirror Feelings?

Your baby is flooded with new experiences, sensations, and emotions. Digestive pain, loud surroundings, growing bones, emerging teeth, and confusing emotions swirling around from the people nearby are all affecting her. She is looking for herself amidst the commotion, and she is working to find a way to integrate this newness. The main way babies learn to see themselves is through the eyes of others. When you connect to your baby and reflect to her what you see happening, it can be orienting for her. With your help, she can find her own center and grow from the inside out.

We all know how wonderful it feels when the person who is caring for us is tuned in and trying to match our feelings. Most people have a deep longing to be seen, heard, and responded to in this kind and gentle way. It is validating and helps us open ourselves to love. This type of respect is important for a positive sense of self. Your baby's sense of self and ability to love grows from feelings of connection and validation.

Babies learn to see themselves through the eyes of others.

C A L M S In Action

Making Contact and Mirroring

Now that Mike has slowed himself down and is able to look at Joshua's experience as something he can interact with, he tries mirroring. He says, "Joshua, sweet boy, I hear that you are upset. I've been feeling anxious and stressed, too." Mike pauses, breathes, and thinks back to his earlier impression of Joshua. He says, "It sounds like you might be feeling pretty overwhelmed." As Joshua looks up and wails at his dad, Mike says, "Yeah, that's hard." Joshua buries his face in his father's chest. Mike pauses for a moment, takes a breath, and says, "I see how you are burrowing your face into my chest. You are safe, and I'm here to protect and take care of you, little guy. Nothing else really matters right now."

As Mike says this, he realizes that his worries at work are less important, and he finds himself totally in the moment with his baby boy. Joshua looks up

CALMS In Action

at Mike, and his crying slows down. He is listening to his father's voice and feeling the settling that his father is experiencing. He is not done crying, but the sounds of his cries are changing. He is starting to pay more attention to Mike and his eyes are open now.

Feeling relieved, relaxed, and hopeful, Anna walks over to join her guys. She says to Joshua, "You seem like you are calming down with your daddy." She turns to Mike, gives him tender kiss and says, "Thank you."

Step 5

C A L M **S**

Soothe Your Baby

Now that you are calmer and connecting with your baby, it is likely that he will be more able to receive and benefit from the comforting measures you have to offer. Usually at this point your baby wants to find a way to stop crying. He has been heard and responded to, and he will be more able to integrate the help he needs to calm down and settle in. He may still need to cycle through the crying again, but now he is doing it with support from you, and you no longer feel like a frustrated, helpless bystander.

S

If your baby is still crying, continue to follow the first four steps of C A L M S—check in with yourself, allow more breaths, listen to your baby, and continue to mirror what he is showing you. Don't despair: crying is one possible normal response to soothing and actually can be very healing. Please trust yourself and your baby, and know that your interactions are meaningful and have a positive effect. Let your infant know that you hear him and understand how upset he is. Know that you have done good work by listening, supporting, and connecting with your baby. You will

Nature, fresh air and a good snuggle have a soothing effect.

find that once he has released his feelings and been heard by you, he may be ready for the soothing you offer and most likely a deep, relaxing sleep. And don't forget that you have been through a lot too, and it is time for some self-care.

How to Soothe

As your child's parent you already have effective tricks and tools for soothing your baby. Here are some simple reminders of the basics:

- Holding
- Breast-feeding or close body contact
- Sweet sounds such as poems or songs
- Being worn in a sling
- Bouncing
- Rocking
- Going outside, feeling fresh air, and seeing plants and animals
- Hearing white noise such as running water or radio static

S

Here are some ideas for how to make your soothing efforts more effective:

- Let your baby know that you are going to try one of the things that usually helps to calm and soothe her.
- Watch her response and notice if she starts the calming and settling.
- Be sure that you are offering, not pushing, the soothing activity onto your baby.
- Continue to listen and reflect as you enter into the soothing activity.
- Give each activity some time for your baby to adapt to it.

It is important to continue your conversation with your baby as you offer soothing behaviors. Let your baby know what you are going to do before you do it, and be sure to continue to observe how your baby is responding. For example, if you offer the breast and your baby is pushing up with her feet, mirror this back to your baby. You might say, "Oh I

Let your baby know what you are doing.

S

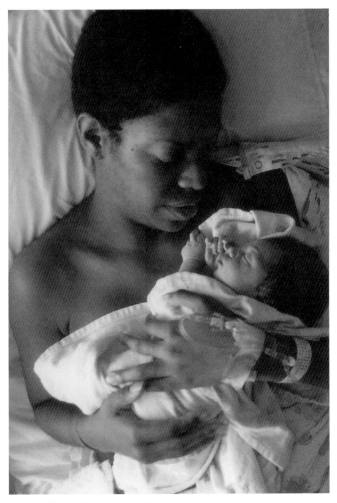

The world is a friendly and safe place.

see you wanting to push," and put your hands on your baby's feet so that she can push against you. She might need some physical movement before she can settle in to feed. Once you begin to notice your baby's cues, you will be more likely to appropriately respond to her communications and meet her needs. It is so important to trust your baby and your own parenting instincts.

Why Soothe?

Although your baby needs to be heard and acknowledged, he also needs to be soothed. All babies are born with very immature nervous systems. During his first several years, your baby relies on you to be his external regulatory system; in other words, he is expecting and needing you to activate his calming responses. Eventually he will learn to do this for himself, but in the beginning he needs help. That is why you feel so compelled to help your baby when he is crying. It's instinctive.

Even though you want to fix everything for your baby, it is not always possible. Sometimes he will simply

S

need to experience his feelings. Being held, cared for, listened to, and acknowledged by a calm, loving person in the midst of intense feelings brings your baby's system back into balance. What you can do is be there and let your baby know that you are trying your best to stay present and connected, and to understand him. When his needs are met, it sends the message to his brain that he is in a world that is friendly and responsive.

CALMS In Action

Soothing

As everyone continues to calm down, Mike notices that Joshua is rooting around on his chest. Anna realizes that it's been about two hours since he has eaten and suggests that she sit down before dinner and offer him some milk. Mike kisses Joshua, hands him to Anna, and tells her that he'll finish cooking dinner. A few minutes later Mike puts dinner on the table, and Joshua is sound asleep in Anna's arms.

Conclusion

Each time that you go through the process of C A L M S, you and your baby will learn more about each other. As a result, you will be more able to soothe and help her through those hard times. As your baby learns that you are there for her when she is struggling, her trust will deepen knowing you will be there for her in every mood and at every turn. This is trust learned at a very deep, essential level in your child's psyche. Because your child is still in a very formative period, the trust learned during this early time is incorporated into her development and becomes a way of being for her. Her experience of your calmness and presence will enhance her ability to be calm and present with herself. With practice, she will become more at ease with your routines and daily activities of her life. This kind of attention will offer your child an emotional foundation of safety and security, and a belief that she lives in a world she can trust.

S

PART TWO

Why Do

C A L M S

❝ The second he came out when he heard Tracy's voice, he picked his head up and looked in her direction and then when I spoke he turned his head and looked in my direction.

—Noah Wyle
Actor narration *What Babies Want*, the movie

In order to fully understand how C A L M S works, it is important to understand this new view of how we unfold as human beings. This perspective comes not only from our own work with families, but from the work of many therapists, researchers, neuroscientists, and teachers past and present. Understanding that babies come into the world as conscious, awake, and aware beings helps us to be kind, gentle, and patient with our young ones.

For a long time our culture has viewed babies in a limited way. Babies were seen as:

- Passive passengers in the womb and for some time after birth.

- Not possessing enough brain structure to express meaningful communication and learn or maintain memories before they are able to speak.

- Unable to experience pain.

- Arriving as a "blank slate."

Now, however, new and exciting knowledge about infants is emerging. Discoveries made in the twentieth and twenty-first centuries in fields such as prenatal psychology, embryology, neurobiology, and attachment theory have changed our world view about babies and human development. We are gaining a much deeper understanding of who babies really are and what they are capable of doing, feeling, knowing, and experiencing.

Children clearly recognize that there is someone inside.

Our current understanding of babies, based on this new perspective, includes the following assumptions:

- Babies are sensitive and aware in the womb and beyond.

- The newborn arrives as a whole person on a lifelong continuum of development.

- Memory is being created through the emotions and the senses from the very beginning.

- Experiences before, during, and after birth have a direct effect on lifelong physical and psychological health.

- A baby's earliest experiences and interactions with parents and caregivers influence how the brain and nervous system develop.

This new recognition of a baby's abilities and sensitivities is teaching us to pay much closer attention to what our babies are thinking and feeling. The indications are that babies are much more cognizant,

Babies are sensitive and aware.

at a much earlier age, than we ever imagined. What we are learning now is that babies are responding, learning, and communicating right from the beginning, and interactive experiences actually stimulate healthy development, especially brain development. This rich expression does not happen in isolation; rather, it is happening in their relationships with parents and caregivers. These exchanges of communication are the foundational building blocks of emotional, physical, and mental well-being. This new understanding offers us an evolutionary way of thinking about and being with babies.

Babies Are People

Your baby is a person. His basic essence is always there, from the beginning of life until the end. Development is the unfolding of his ability to express what is already present and active in him from the beginning. When you look at your newborn baby, you may be taken with how vulnerable he seems. His physical abilities are so limited that it might be easy to overlook the big being in the little body. During these early days, you might be more aware of the ways he is different from you, but there are also many ways that he is the same. For example, he is unable to speak, but he finds ways of communicating. He cannot feed himself, but he shows you when he is hungry. He cannot move from place to place without your assistance right now, but soon he will be moving around on his own.

Your baby's brain and body are working as fast as they can to develop in order to give him the freedom to express himself in ways you will be able to understand, and to express who he really is and what he is here to do in this world. Within weeks after birth he will be laughing and smiling. Within months he will be moving around on his own. Within a year he will be eating most of the foods that you eat, and within two years he will be running around and working toward speaking in sentences. If you watch your baby, you will see that even now he is working really hard to master all of these skills.

Once you realize that your baby is a whole person, it changes the way you interact with him and enhances his ability to be himself in the world. You include him in the conversations. You attribute more importance to his needs. You think about how your actions are affecting him, and you respect him more fully.

Nature and Nurture

The question of nature versus nurture has long been debated in an effort to understand how humans develop. What determines who we will become: our essential nature and our genes, or our environment? Currently many researchers agree that human development is an ongoing interplay between nature and nurture. Our essential nature and our genetics provide us with a core of being. This is the nature part of life. As we grow, we develop a network of nerves that connect our brain structure, and our body systems mature under the influence of environmental pressure. This is the nurture part of life.

The core of being is potent and alive with possibility.

The core of being is potent and alive with possibility. It is our deepest part, and it forms what we identify as self. Your baby comes into the world already trying to express herself in every way that she can. At birth she is limited by physical ability, which must be somewhat frustrating. Even so, right from the beginning, your baby is expressing herself and letting you know who she is. Her character, preferences, and general approach to life are all visible if you know what to look for. Most parents will say that when they look into the eyes of their new baby they can see that this baby is her own person, different from all others they have known. This might be describing the nature aspect of a person.

The effect of the environment and the care your baby receives is the nurture aspect of life. This part of her development helps her formulate her ability to express her inner nature. The nurture aspect includes the influence of the environment and relationships. The way you nurture your baby profoundly influences how she uses her body and mind to connect with the world and to be a part of your family and the human family. This begins during gestation when a baby's experiences are filtered through her mother. At birth she begins to experience the environment more directly but continues to rely on her mother for cues about the environment. She also connects with and deepens relationships with the people close to her.

We believe that nature is the core, the essence of who each child is, and nurture is the way parents can support their children to be able to express the qualities that they come into the world with.

Babies Are Sensing

Your baby emerged from the womb as an extraordinarily sensitive being. He uses all of his senses (sight, smell, sound, taste, and touch) to learn about his environment. During the early months before he can speak, this sensing is the way he gathers information about the world in which he lives.

For most babies, the world is a very busy, bright, and noisy place. Over time we, as adults, have learned to tune out a lot of what is going on around us. Because your baby is so sensitive and open to learning, he cannot do that yet. As a result, if the environment is overly stimulating, for example, the lights are too bright or there is too much noise, your baby may become overwhelmed. When this happens, he will often let you know by crying or just shutting down and going to sleep until things are more at a level he can manage. When you are able to tune in to your baby's unique tolerance for sensory stimulation, it is very supportive to his well-being. Bringing him slowly and willingly into the outside world will help his nervous system to integrate what he is experiencing.

Babies Learn How to Make Sense of Their Feelings From the People Who Care For Them

Because your baby cannot yet assess the outside world very well, she will tune in to the one thing she knows—you. Your baby will sense if things are safe or unsafe, happy or sad, or fun or dangerous by tuning in to your emotional state and responding based on your reactions.

Your baby will sense if things are fun or dangerous by tuning in to you.

To illustrate this point, imagine walking into a room and seeing someone you love. You can often sense how that person is feeling. This sensing is commonly referred to as a "gut feeling" or intuition; it is a way of knowing, a way of tuning in, and resonating to the emotional state of another person. All humans are capable of this. Your baby is extra sensitive to how others are feeling because her sense of their feelings lets her know if she is physically and emotionally safe in any given situation.

Because of this sensing by your baby, the first step in the C A L M S protocol is checking in with yourself. If you are upset, stressed, hopeless, sad, or angry, your baby will be able to sense this and be affected by those feelings. If, at this stage, you spend a few moments relaxing your body and mind, your baby will soon learn this routine. This is especially important when you are responding to your baby when she is upset. If you approach her with anxiety or alarm, she will sense your reaction and express even more distress. However, if you check in and take a moment to settle yourself she will sense that and will take your cue that all is well, she is safe, and she can calm down.

By repeating this action you have the chance to give your baby the gift early in life of learning how to calm and settle during stressful times. The behaviors your baby learns at this stage will become second nature to her throughout her life. You certainly can't avoid all stress or difficult feelings, but you can help your baby learn how to manage them effectively right from the start by being mindful of how you are feeling when you are caring for your baby.

Sorting Out Feelings

It can be a little disconcerting to think that your baby is so tuned in to you. This does not mean that you always have to be perfect and on guard: your baby can also tell when you are trying to mask your feelings. It's more helpful to be honest and open about your feelings.

When you check in with yourself, you can name and own your feelings. Let your baby know in a simple

Let go of stress and tune into what is happening in the present.

way what is happening. By taking this step your baby will be free from having to worry about things that are not appropriate for him. You might say something like, "I am upset because I bounced a check, but that doesn't have anything to do with you and I can handle it. I am not upset with you, and we are safe." Even though your baby doesn't understand bouncing checks, your explanation will carry a shift in energy as you own your stress.

The added bonus of naming your situation out loud for your baby is that it can give you a sense of perspective about the problem as well. One of the great things we can learn from being with a baby is to be in this moment, right here, right now. When we take our cues from the baby, we begin to let go of stress and just attend to what is happening in the present. You can still deal with that bounced check—and even be upset or annoyed by it—but the key is to not let that interfere with your emotional interactions with your baby.

Babies Experience Birth

Now that we know how sensitive and aware babies are, birth from the baby's perspective takes on a new meaning. During birth, babies go through an intense transition. No matter how your baby is born, the journey to the outside world is profound, resulting in numerous internal and external changes. For example, at birth, every one of your baby's senses, especially her skin, is exposed to new and heightened stimuli. Your baby immediately begins to breathe on her own, using her lungs for the first time, which changes the way her heart circulates blood. When we hold her with the knowledge that she is aware and making an enormous transition, it helps her feel safe.

The way your baby is cared for and welcomed at birth can have a big influence on how she adjusts to the outside environment. Your baby is born with instincts and reflexes that are intended to help her survive—the strongest of which is the desire and will to connect with her mother. At birth she knows to look for her mother's face and is able to recognize

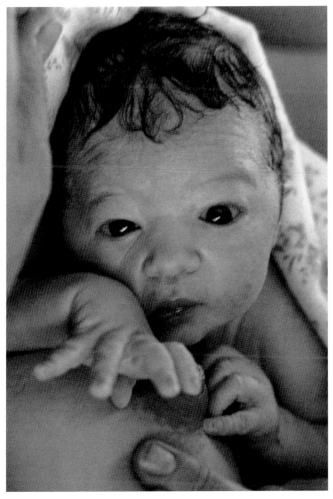

Just minutes old, and wide awake.

her mother's voice, touch, and scent. Just like any other baby mammal, your baby is born with reflexes that will help her connect her to her mother. She has crawling reflexes that will help her move to the breast, and she has rooting and sucking reflexes to help her find the breast and latch on. When she is placed on her mother at birth, she has the experience of having her instinctual needs fulfilled. This, in turn, helps her feel safe and secure.

Security is everything to a baby.

What Do Babies Want?

Imagine what it would be like to be sensitive and aware of what is happening around you and at the same time physically helpless—unable to get to what you need, go where you want, or tell people how you are feeling. How would you want to be cared for? How would you like the people around you to communicate with you? How would you want to be treated?

Putting yourself in this position will give you a window into the experience your baby is having. He is a person with thoughts, feelings, and needs, yet he cannot express himself in ways that others can easily understand. This is such a vulnerable time of life for your child. What he wants most during this time is to feel safe, loved, and respected as a human being. When people are respectful toward us we feel seen, heard, and valued. Just like us, this is what babies want.

Let's look at some of the ways you are giving your baby what he wants. Physical touch is the best way to communicate safety and love to a brand-new person. When you hold, snuggle, and massage your little one regularly during the day, you are letting him know that you are there and will keep him out of harm's way. Sustained skin-to-skin contact helps build his brain and strengthen all of his vital body systems. Your physical presence is a great way to reassure your baby that all is well. Another way is to verbally communicate directly with your baby. When you verbally reflect what you sense your baby is feeling, you are connecting. Telling your baby what you will be doing with him throughout the course of the day helps your baby feel safe and cared for. When you include your baby in the conversations you are having, especially if you are speaking about him, you are showing him respect.

Your Baby's Developing Mind

Your baby senses both your physical and emotional presence. In order to fully understand this we need to look at early brain development. By the end of the first trimester, your baby has developed all of the parts of her brain; the next step is to connect all of these parts together. This miraculous connection process

Skin to skin contact helps build her brain.

occurs throughout life but is most significant during the last few months of gestation and the first three years of childhood. This connecting process does not happen on its own; rather, it is directly linked to our relationships and interactions with our caregivers. As the brain connects through interaction with other humans, it begins to create meaning. With meaning, your baby begins to form a neurological map of her unique world.

In order for your baby to be able to form a strong connection to you, which in turn will influence the healthy development of her brain, it is vital that you learn to perceive and respond to your child's experience and emotional state. In the film What Babies Want, well-known author and teacher, Joseph Chilton Pearce says, "You don't have to teach the child emotional intelligence; you have to be it around them. You can't keep the brain from absorbing it." This is why, in the case of stressful experiences, it is useful for the caregiver to be able to take a calming moment. Your baby responds to stress, and if you can calm down, your baby will copy your behavior and incorporate it, actually hardwiring it into her neural structures. It may take many times of consistently doing this, but your baby will learn and benefit. You are teaching your baby how to work through stressful situations.

What You Can Do With Feelings of Frustration

It is three o'clock in the morning, and your baby has woken up crying every hour for the past three hours. You are jarred out of sleep, feeling exhausted, and unable to cope. As a new parent, there may be times when you feel frustrated, angry, or helpless. It can be very challenging when your baby is crying inconsolably, not sleeping well, having trouble breastfeeding, or just simply growing. Remember, your baby is new at this, too. It is important to let your baby know that your feelings of frustration are about the circumstances of the situation and not about him.

Just as important as it is to support your baby, you need support, too. If you are sleep-deprived and struggling, reach out to trusted friends and relations.

Humans are social creatures.

It is fine for us to suggest that you just take a breath and relax, but you might need a friend to lean on in order to be able to get your breath! As a new parent you deserve support and help, and should not be expected (or expect yourself) to do everything alone. First, try to lower your expectations of what you think you should get done each day, and nap with your baby. Then, take care of yourself—call a friend, find an online chat group, or connect with a parenting resource center in your town. It helps to talk about your frustrations and challenges, and to know that others are struggling with similar issues.

Community Support

Humans are social creatures. These days, with families scattered across the globe, it is important to establish a group of friends and spend time with them. Parents of young children especially benefit from being with other parents. It is very helpful to know that you are not the only one who is sleep-deprived, confused, or frustrated with the challenges of early parenthood.

Often other moms and dads have helpful tips and coping skills that can be useful.

It is also important to build relationships with people who understand and are going through similar experiences. Having that level of support on a regular basis is not only very affirming, but actually helps settle and release tension and anxiety, which will help your baby remain calm and settled as well.

When the greater community welcomes your baby and family, it creates a sense of love and security for everyone. Society needs children as much as children need society. Our children represent the future. Being part of a multigenerational community who acknowledge children can make a huge difference for the health of the community. Babies and children want to be in a world where they are welcomed, can express themselves, and be recognized and honored for who they are. Trust your child, believe that her communications are valid, and respond to her in the way that you would like to be responded to. Each human comes into this world with a purpose, a reason for being here. When we see our children this way, they are supported to fulfill their purpose for being here. Recognition and respect from family and community gives them the precious gift of self-worth.

Community elders welcome a new baby at the farmers market.

Conclusion

The C A L M S Steps have come a long way from when we first conceived them. What started out as a simple protocol for being with a crying baby has turned into a basic template to use in good times as well as in the more challenging times. People have adapted these steps to meet their family needs, keeping the basic premise of respectful communication at the center.

As parents, we all want to raise children who are independent, trusting, and trustworthy. From the very beginning, we start to do the things we think will mold the child in that direction, and very often we end up parenting as our parents did, even though we promised we wouldn't. The C A L M S steps call for a new approach and one that is not always easy to follow. In the end, it requires that we make personal changes, work on healing our own wounds, and come into greater personal balance.

Independence in a child comes with time. In the natural way of things, it is appropriate for a child to start out dependent. Sometimes we are in such a hurry for our kids to demonstrate their independence that we forget to give them time to develop independence authentically from the center of their being, in small steps in the beginning of their lives. Every child has a strong inner drive to be herself, to stand on her own, and to speak her truth. It is the same inner drive that causes her to learn language and the motor skills to stand up and balance on her own two feet. For a truly independent child, the first step is to hold her close, give her every assurance of love and care, and meet her infantile needs. With this solid, loving foundation, she will gradually become more confident of her independence in her own time. It is up to you to follow her early cues for both dependence and independence. Fulfill her developmental needs, and then let go and watch her fly!

Much of the same can be said for trust. When we use the C A L M S steps to connect with our children from the start, we show them trust in the most fundamental of ways. We show them that their needs have value and will be met most of the time. We show them that when they express themselves, we will be here to hear them, and when they are afraid or need help, we are here to support them. A child who has been welcomed warmly into the world by family and friends, and who has been met with love and respect, will have developed a core belief that the world is a good place. She will believe that she can do well and that life is beautiful.

You want your child to grow and develop into a child you can trust. We think that trustworthy children come from parents who trust and believe in them, parents who accept their children's communications as genuine, and who respond to them with heart. When your child starts out with a brain that has formed in the context of respect and connection, she will be trustworthy. At every challenging time of her development, you will find that you do not have to lose contact with her to be able to take charge of the next layer of life. You are in cooperation with each other, and developmental stages like the "terrible twos" and the teen years will take on new and amazing dimensions. You will find that your child's behavior is appropriate, and her independence is gratifying to you. When you maintain respectful communication with your child, you will respect each other, trust each other, and be trustworthy. You will find that you have established a life-long relationship based on love and mutual respect.

This is the greatest blessing one can have in life, and we wish for this amazing experience of parenting to be your experience as well.

PART THREE

Parenting
Questions & Answers

❝ We cannot prepare for the future without embracing
the meaning and the relevance of the baby's
perspective on life.

—Michel Odent, M.D.
Obstetrician, author

We hope this book has opened your eyes to a new way of thinking about your baby and that you are feeling inspired to find your way toward creating a deep and connected lifelong relationship with your beautiful child.

The purpose of the C A L M S method is to give you a way of "being with" yourself and your child, no matter what style of parenting you are using.

Now that you have read the book we are going to offer you a series of common questions and answers that parents have about using the C A L M S method.

Checking in with myself does not come naturally. Will I ever get the hang of it?

First and foremost, give yourself a break. For most of us this is a new skill. You might not get it right away. In fact, it might feel awkward and unnatural for a little while. Like learning any new skill, it takes time and patience, and a lot of self-love and appreciation.

Consider it like learning a new instrument. You have to practice before you become proficient, but the more you practice, the easier it will become. After a while, it will feel like second nature. One way to start honing the skill of checking in is to pick one or more times during the day when you consciously ask yourself, "How am I feeling? What sensations do I notice in my body?" You might do this when waking in the morning or as you are falling asleep at night. Another good time is when you sit down to nurse or feed your baby. Creating the habit of checking in with yourself takes time but is well worth the effort.

Sometimes when I check in with myself I don't believe what I am sensing. How can I get to what I'm really feeling?

When people are learning the step of checking in, it is common that they get a sense of something that they are feeling, and then doubt or deny it. It really helps to trust yourself and to trust your feelings even if they are uncomfortable. Just as when you are listening for your baby's feelings, it helps if you accept what comes up. If it's not what was expected, be honest and curious about it. If you are having trouble figuring out what you are feeling, ask yourself, "Am I feeling scared, angry, frustrated, disappointed, resentful?" Give yourself some choices and see which emotion resonates.

Sometimes when I check in with myself I realize that I am feeling angry and resentful. What do I do with those feelings?

Ask any parent and you will realize that you are not alone. These are normal feelings that tend to arise when we feel overwhelmed and stressed. Giving yourself time to calm down is way more beneficial to you and your baby than trying to parent from an angry or frustrated place.

During this time it's extra important to practice the second step of C A L M S —allow a breath. This step is about doing whatever it takes to slow down and come back to the present moment. If the feelings of frustration and resentment are there, you can't just wish them away or step around them. Acknowledge what you are feeling, and do what you can to move through the emotions—take deep breaths, slowly drink a big glass of water, walk into another room, or go outside and get some fresh air. If you practice self-care and the feelings of frustration or anger continue to come, you may need more help. Be willing to ask for support from a friend or family member or possibly seek counseling.

I try taking breaths to center myself but it doesn't work. Is there something wrong with me?

Just like checking in with yourself, this may be a new skill. Be patient and practice often. Start becoming more aware of taking breaths when you are not particularly stressed. If you feel like breathing is not your best tool for calming yourself down right now, try to find other things that work better for you. More and more studies are pointing out that nature has a balancing effect on us. Find a view, a place outside, or even a house plant you can connect with. Another calming elixir is water. Drink it, splash it on your face, wash your hands, or take a shower or bath. There is no right way to slow yourself down; the key is to find what works for you.

I feel like there is no time to attend to myself first when my baby needs me because it feels wrong to let my baby cry even for a little while. How do I deal with that?

Of course it is difficult to hear your baby cry. It's completely natural and appropriate to want to attend to her needs as soon as she shows signs of being upset. What we are suggesting is that when you hear her cry, before you react, take a very brief pause to notice how you are feeling. This will allow you to slow down before attending to your baby. The first two steps of C A L M S —checking in and allowing a breath—can be done in less than ten seconds. Taking just ten seconds to collect yourself before you attend to your baby will allow you and your baby to calm down sooner. Ultimately, you will have an easier time calming her down and she will spend far less time upset. Think of it as a small investment in everyone's long-term well-being.

The third step of CALMS is to listen. I listen but I still don't know what my baby is saying. Now what?

In the beginning, it is very normal to feel like you do not know what your baby is communicating. The point of listening to your baby in the early weeks and months is to communicate your presence, to allow your child to feel that you are interested in knowing him, and to try to understand what he is telling you. Be patient. You are getting to know this new person who speaks a different language and has a different story.

Over time you will learn what your baby is saying. And in doing so, you will have laid the foundation for a very healthy and trusting relationship.

What if I think I know what my baby is saying and I try to help him but it doesn't work? Can you address what happens if you incorrectly interpret what your baby is saying?

In the process of communication, misunderstandings are common. It's normal and happens to everybody.

Remember that the listening and mirroring steps of C A L M S are intended to be repeated. Think of this as a process of discovery. Just like in all relationships, you might not understand what your baby is trying to tell you all of the time. Do your best, try things, and trust that your baby will give you feedback on how you are doing. Even if your baby is still crying after you responded, you might not have been completely wrong. Watch your baby's shifting responses to your words and see if you can refine your understanding.

It is also possible that you may have perceived the communication clearly and your baby wants you to know more about his feelings. Keep listening. Keep reflecting. Try different things. Your baby is not looking for perfection, just connection.

There are times when I understand what my baby wants, but I can't do it right away. What can I do?

This will happen; you are human. During these times it's helpful if you can acknowledge that you understand that your baby wants something; then tell your baby what you are feeling or needing to do instead. For example, it might be obvious that your baby is ready to eat because she is rooting and starting to squawk and cry out. When you check in with yourself, you notice that you have to go to the bathroom. At this point it is better for you to take care of your own need first and then take care of your baby. You might say, "Dear one, I know you are hungry and ready to eat, but before I can feed you, I must go to the bathroom." Your baby will probably cry until you start to feed her. That's okay, especially if you or someone else is available to tell your baby that you understand she is hungry and ready to eat. When you return you can let your baby know that you really heard her and are ready to feed her for a good long while.

When my baby cries, all I can think of is what can I do to make him feel better. Why should I mirror his feelings when I can just soothe him?

When your baby feels upset, yes, he does want you to help him feel better, but before you offer soothing, he wants to know that you understand how he is feeling. Here's an example that will illustrate this point. Imagine you are really upset and you have a strong need to tell someone you love about what is happening. You go to your best friend for support. She takes one look at you, puts her arm around your shoulders and says, "Wow, I see that you are really sad, tell me all about it." This makes you cry even harder because you sense that she really wants to hear about what you are feeling. After a little while of her sitting with you calmly, you slow down enough to tell her why you are upset. She listens and assures you that she hears what you are telling her. Next, she offers you a glass of water. You drink the water and notice that you are feeling much better because you have been able to express your feelings to someone who was able to be present with you while you were upset.

Now, imagine the same scenario, but this time you go to a friend who is not quite so relaxed. You walk in crying, and she says, "Oh, you are going to be just fine. Here, have a drink. You're okay; don't worry about it." You sense that she does not really want to hear what you have to say. You might stop crying but it is likely that you will not feel settled by this friend's actions.

Which type of care would you prefer? Our point is that when your baby is upset he needs to feel that you are with him and that you are empathizing with his state before you try to move him beyond that experience. At times you may find that your baby won't let you soothe him. This is often a strong signal that he may need you to settle yourself more and listen to what he has to say.

I feel silly talking to my baby. How can I become more comfortable with it?

We understand that at first it might feel awkward or odd to talk to your baby, but the more you do it the easier it becomes. Eventually talking to your baby will feel natural.

It's important to tune in to your baby. When your baby is engaged with you, tell her about where you are going, what you are doing, and the things you are seeing. She will appreciate the contact. Even if she is not engaged, it is still courteous to give her the heads-up on what is happening around her, especially in the midst of transitions or when things are going to be done to her body. When she is relaxed, be mindful of slowing down and letting her have space to just be. Babies are often happy to have connection without a lot of words, especially when they are with the people they love. Trust that you will have a sense of when it's time to talk or when it's just time to be.

How do I get a conversation going with my baby?

The idea of having a conversation with a young baby may be new to most people. When your baby is in a quiet but awake state, hold him about twelve inches from your face, check in with yourself, take a few breaths and settle yourself. As you are doing this, start to notice what your baby may be experiencing. Next, say a few words about what is happening, and then relax, wait, and see what your baby does. Mirror back to your baby what you see or hear him doing. Again, pause, relax, and see what he expresses. When you let your baby know what you are hearing from him, your baby will respond to that. Be open! His communication may come in the form of a wiggle, an arm raise, a facial expression, or a sound. Just notice and say what you see. By noticing, you are having a conversation. Try it for three to five minutes at a time. Each time you do this you will get more insight into your baby's world.

If I've done the steps of CALMS, and I've tried to soothe my baby but she still won't stop crying. Am I doing something wrong?

Not necessarily. Because she doesn't have the brain structures and neural pathways to filter out excess input, she can get wound up and overwhelmed more easily than you can. Sometimes crying is an expression of "I just have too much going on right now. Wah!"

Whether she is overwhelmed, has a stomachache (and sometimes these go together), or just feels out of sorts, your baby needs to have you there while she is having her feelings. Obviously, it's important to check to see if your baby is hungry, wet, hot, cold, or physically uncomfortable. However, if there is no consoling her, stay with her, repeat the C A L M S steps, and let her know that you are there for her. As you learn to do the C A L M S steps in situations like these, you are giving your baby the support she needs.

Intellectually I understand that sometimes my baby needs to cry but there are times when I can't handle it. What should I do?

There will be times when you feel like you just don't have it in you to calm your baby down. If you have another adult with you, such as a partner or friend, let that person know you need a break. Give your helper a minute to transition, and let your baby know what is happening. If you are alone with your baby, tell him that you are having a tough time, put him somewhere safe, and take some steps to calm yourself down. Let him know what you are doing and when you will be back. Remember to tell your baby each step of the way what is happening. If you are getting overwhelmed regularly, get help.

There may be times when you and your baby need to change the scene. Put him in a carrier or the stroller, or just hold him and get out of the house. Getting out into nature is a great way to help you and your baby shift out of a very upset state. If you can't leave the house, you may run a bath or take some time to lay down on the bed with your baby. Yes, it's important to listen to your baby when he is upset and sometimes it's also important to help him shift by offering a change of scenery. If you think that your baby is sick or in pain, consult your doctor right away.

Acknowledgments

This book would not have been possible without the love, support and encouragement from so many people.

We are grateful to our teachers and mentors—Marti Glenn, Phyllis Klaus, Wendy Anne McCarty, Ray Castellino, David Chamberlain, William Emerson, Thomas Verny, Barbara Findeisen, John Chitty, Michael Shea, and so many other incredible people who have inspired us along the way.

To our friends and colleagues who read the manuscript and contributed suggestions—Erica Holten, Karen Strange, Bernadette Noll, Jodi Egerton, Noey Turk, Ky Takikawa, Sally Carricaburu, Annie Yakutis.

To Stephanie Croff for her soothing sense of design & typographic touch.

To the photographers and the families who appear in the photos. Their presence has deepened the meaning of our words.

And to our family members for their love and support throughout the writing process, and the innumerable babies, children, and parents we have worked with who have shared their wisdom with us.

References

Section Two

Chamberlain, David. *The Mind of Your Newborn Baby*. Berkeley, CA: North Atlantic Books, 1998.

Klaus, Marshall and Phyllis Klaus. *Your Amazing Newborn*. Cambridge, MA: Perseus Books, 1999.

Lipton, Bruce. *The Biology of Belief: Unleashing the Power of Consciousness, Matter and Miracles*. Santa Rosa, CA: Mountain of Love/Elite Books, 2005.

McCarty, Wendy Anne. *Welcoming Consciousness: Supporting Babies' Wholeness From the Beginning of Life*. Goleta, CA: Wondrous Beginnings, 2004.

Somé, Sobonfu. *Welcoming Spirit Home: Ancient African Teachings to Celebrate Children and Community*. Novato, CA: New World Library, 1999.

Takikawa, Debby. DVD *What Babies Want*. Los Olivos, CA: Hana Peace Works, 2004.

Verny, Thomas and John Kelly. *The Secret Life of the Unborn Child: How You Can Prepare Your Baby for a Happy Healthy, Life*. New York: Summit Books, 1981.

Additional References

Buckley, Sarah. *Gentle Birth, Gentle Mothering: A Doctor's Guide to Natural Childbirth and Gentle Early Parenting Choices.* Berkeley, CA: Celestial Arts, 2009.

Castillino, Raymond. "The Stress Matrix: Implications for Prenatal and Birth Therapy." *Journal of Prenatal & Perinatal Psychology & Health* 15, 1 (2000), 31–62.

Emerson, William. *Treating Birth Trauma During Infancy.* Dynamic Outcomes, Petaluma, CA: Emerson Training Seminars, 1996.

Gerhardt, Sue. *Why Love Matters: How Affection Shapes a Babies Brain.* East Sussex, England: Brunner-Rutledge, 2004.

Greenspan, Stanley I. *The Growth of the Mind: And the Endangered Origins of Intelligence.* Reading, MA: Addison-Wesley Pub., 1997.

Grille, Robin. *Parenting For a Peaceful World.* Sydney, Australia: Longueville Media, 2005.

Karen, Robert. *Becoming Attached: Unfolding the Mystery of the Infant-Mother Bond and Its Impact on Later Life.* New York: Warner Books, 1994.

Klaus, Marshall, Joh Kennell, and Phyllis Klaus. *Bonding: Building the Foundation of Secure Attachment and Independence.* Reading, MA: Addison-Wesley Publishing Co., 1995.

LeDoux, Joseph. *The Emotional Brain: The Mysterious Underpinnings of Emotional Life.* New York, NY: Simon and Schuster, 1996.

Levine, Peter A. *Waking the Tiger: The Innate Capacity to Transform Overwhelming Experiences.* Berkeley, CA: North Atlantic Books, 1997.

Lewis, Thomas, Fari Amini, and Richard Lannon. *A General Theory of Love.* New York, NY: Random House, 2000.

Mehrabian, Albert, and Susan R. Ferris, "Inference of Attitudes from Nonverbal Communication in Two Channels." *Journal of Consulting Psychology* 31, 3 (1967): 248–252.

Mitchell, Rachel. L. C., Rebecca Elliott, Martin. Barry, Alan Crittenden, and Peter W. R. Woodruff. "The Neural Response to Emotional Prosody, as Revealed by Functional Magnetic Resonance Imaging." *Neuropsychologia* 41 (2003): 1410–1421.

Nugent, J. Kevin, Constance H. Keefer, Susan Minear, et al. *Understanding Newborn Behavior and Early Relationships: The Newborn Behavioral Observations Handbook.* Baltimore, MD: Paul H. Brookes Publishing Company, 2007.

Orlinsky, David E., and K. I. Howard, "Process and Outcome in Psychotherapy." In *Handbook of Psychotherapy and Behavior Change (3rd ed.),* edited by Sol. Louis. Garfield and Allan E. Bergin. New York: Wiley, 1986.

Pearce, Joseph Chilton. *Magical Child: Rediscovering Nature's Plan for our Children.* New York, NY: Dutton, 1997.

Shea, Michael J. *Biodynamic Craniosacral Therapy,* Volume Two. Berkeley, CA: North Atlantic Books, 2007–2008.

Shore, Allan. *Affect Regulation and the Origins of the Self: The Neurobiology of Emotional Development*. Hillsdale, NJ: Lawrence Erlbaum Associates Inc., 1994.

Shore, Allan. *Affect Regulation and the Origins of the Self: The Neurobiology of Emotional Development*. Hillsdale, NJ: Lawrence Erlbaum Associates Inc., 1994.

Siegel, Daniel and Mary Hartzell. *Parenting From the Inside Out: How a Deeper Self-Understanding Can Help You Raise Children Who Thrive*. New York, NY: J. P. Tarcher/Putnam, 2004.

Siegel, Daniel. *The Developing Mind: How Relationships and the Brain Interact to Shape Who We Are*. New York, NY: Guilford Press, 1999.

Sunderland, Margot. *The Science of Parenting: Practical Guidance on Sleep, Crying, Play, and Building Emotional Well-Being for Life*. New York, NY: Doring Kindersley Publishing, 2006.

About the Photographer

 **Fran Collin** is an acclaimed advertising, editorial, and fine art photographer. His work has been published and shown internationally. We are so grateful for his commitment to the photos in this book and for his sensitive and understanding view of mothers, fathers, and babies. Fran and his wife, Denise, have a daughter Sofia.

www.francollin.com; www.work-for-food.com

Photo Credits

The photos Fran did not take are listed below.

About the Authors

Carrie Contey, PhD, is a nationally recognized coach, consultant, speaker, educator and the co-founder of Slow Family Living. Her background offers a unique perspective on children, parenting, family life and what it means to be a healthy, happy, whole human being.

photo © Leon Alesi

Carrie guides, supports and inspires her clients to live with a wide-open and courageous heart so that they can approach parenting, and life, with both skill and spaciousness. Carrie lives, works and plays in Austin, TX. To learn more please visit www.carriecontey.com.

Debby Takikawa, DC, A doctor of chiropractic by formal

education, Debby Takikawa trained in the field of prenatal and infant psychology with Ray Castellino at the BEBA Clinic in Santa Barbara California. She then went on to form the nonprofit organization, Beginnings, Inc. A Resource Center for Children and Families. The mission of the clinic was to serve babies, children and their families challenged by attachment issues, birth trauma, and other health concerns. The clinic was also a teaching facility and had a mandate for public outreach and education. It was through this arm of the nonprofit that Debby made the documentary film, *What Babies Want (www.whatbabieswant.com).*

C A L M S is the result of Debby and Carrie Contey joining forces to address questions parents asked after watching the film.

Reducing Infant Mortality is Debby's most recent film and can be seen and downloaded for free under the creative commons license at www.reducinginfantmortality.com.

Debby lives on an organic flower and vegetable farm in Los Olivos California with her husband and her extended family.

Photo © Emily Payne

Step 1
Check in With Yourself

The first step in calming your crying baby is to check in with yourself, take a pause and identify your own feelings.

Step 2
Allow a Breath

Take several deep breaths and allow things to simply be just as they are in this moment.

Step 3
Listen to Your Baby

Take a moment or two just to wonder what you think your baby is trying to say.

Step 4
Make Contact and Mirror Feelings

Let your baby know you hear him and you see that he is sad or angry, frustrated or frantic.

Step 5
Soothe Your Baby

Now is the time to do the rocking, walking, swaddling, breastfeeding and soothing that wasn't working earlier.

What Babies Want

An Exploration of the Consciousness of Infants

A Documentary by **Debby Takikawa**
Narrated by **Noah Wyle**

This award-winning documentary film explores the profoundly important and sacred opportunity of bringing children into the world.

To Order:
800 893-5070
whatbabieswant.com

Featuring

Ray Castellino, David Chamberlain, Barbara Findeisen, Marti Glenn, Jay Gordon
Mary Jackson, Wendy Ann McCarty, Joseph Chilton Pearce, Sobonu Somé

Run Time **58 min.** Available in VHS & DVD

C

Step 1
Check in With Yourself

The first step in calming your crying baby is to check in with yourself, take a pause and identify your own feelings.

A

Step 2
Allow a Breath

Take several deep breaths and allow things to simply be just as they are in this moment.

L

Step 3
Listen to Your Baby

Take a moment or two just to wonder what you think your baby is trying to say.

M

Step 4
Make Contact and Mirror Feelings

Let your baby know you hear him and you see that he is sad or angry, frustrated or frantic.

S

Step 5
Soothe Your Baby

Now is the time to do the rocking, walking, swaddling, breastfeeding and soothing that wasn't working earlier.

A *What Babies Want* Parenting Book

❝ What I really like about the C A L M S approach to interacting with your baby is that it crosses all parenting styles. Whatever your parenting method is, these ideas can help you build a more conscious and connected relationship with your infant.❞

—Katharine
mother of two

Debby
whatbabieswant.com

Available from

Hana Peace Works
PO Box 681, Los Olivos, CA 93441

800 893-5070

www.whatbabieswant.com

Carrie
carrie@carriecontey.com

Notes

Notes

Notes

" What I like about the C A L M S approach to interacting with your baby is that it crosses all parenting styles. No matter if you are co-sleeping or crib-sleeping, bottle feeding or breastfeeding, a working mom/dad or a stay-at-home mom/dad, these ideas can help everyone build a more conscious and connected relationship with their infant.

—Katharine
mother of two

" This book is user-friendly and a little life-saver for Moms and Dads as they embark upon the grand journey of caring for their child. It will help you inject peace, harmony and pleasure into your relationship with your child. The beautiful and heart-warming family photos sprinkled throughout will keep you connected to our larger human family.

—Robin Grille
Author of *Parenting for a Peaceful World*

" C A L M S offers parents a reassuring guide to effectively connect with their babies when they need it most. It starts at the beginning and brings in the important elements of connection.

—Wendy Anne McCarty, PhD
Author of *Being With Babies: What Babies are Teaching Us* and
Welcoming Consciousness